AMD

I0820988

AMD

ODYSSEYS

ERIN SILVER

CREATIVE EDUCATION · CREATIVE PAPERBACKS

Published by Creative Education and Creative Paperbacks
P.O. Box 227, Mankato, Minnesota 56002
Creative Education and Creative Paperbacks are imprints of
The Creative Company
www.thecreativecompany.us

Design by Blue Design
Art direction by Tom Morgan

Images by Dreamstime/Aleksei Gorodenkov, 8, Andreistanescu, 20; Getty Images/Alessio Morgese/NurPhoto, 75, David Paul Morris/Bloomberg, 61, Feng Li, 46, Grabowsky/ullstein bild, 12, MediaNews Group/The Mercury News, 16, Nathan Howard/Bloomberg, 50, Sergio Flores/Bloomberg, 67, Smith Collection/Gado, 57, Ted Streshinsky Photographic Archive, 19; Pexels/Andrey Matveev, 70, Nicolas Foster, cover; Reich Ministry of Public Enlightenment and Propaganda, 49; Wikimedia Commons/Akos Kokai, 54, AMD Global, 2, AT&T photographer Jack St., 28, Coolcaesar, 4–5, -EMR, 69, FritzchensFritz, 6, 58, Fuzheado, 24, Gene Wang, 32–33, JPC24M, 42, NASA, 26, Oak Ridge National Laboratory, 62, Tainan City Government, 37, U.S. Department of Energy, 11

Library of Congress Cataloging-in-Publication Data

Names: Silver, Erin, 1980- author
Title: AMD / Erin Silver.
Description: Mankato, Minnesota : Creative Education and Creative Paperbacks, [2026] | Series: Odysseys in business | Includes bibliographical references and index. | Audience: Ages 12-15 | Audience: Grades 7-9 | Summary: "Uncover AMD's breakthroughs in processors and graphics technology. High-school age learners will explore how this tech giant reshaped gaming, AI, and computing, inspiring the next generation of engineers and innovators. This title includes sidebars, a glossary, selected bibliography, websites, and an index"— Provided by publisher.
Identifiers: LCCN 2025021157 (print) | LCCN 2025021158 (ebook) | ISBN 9798895811337 library binding | ISBN 9798896800866 paperback | ISBN 9798895812594 ebook
Subjects: LCSH: Advanced Micro Devices (Firm)—Juvenile literature | Semiconductor industry—United States--Juvenile literature | Microelectronics industry—United States--Juvenile literature.
Classification: LCC HD9696.S44 A3885 2026 (print) | LCC HD9696.S44 (ebook) | DDC 338.4/7621381520973—dc23/eng/20250530
LC record available at https://lccn.loc.gov/2025021157
LC ebook record available at https://lccn.loc.gov/2025021158

Printed in the United States

AMD

AMD
RYZEN

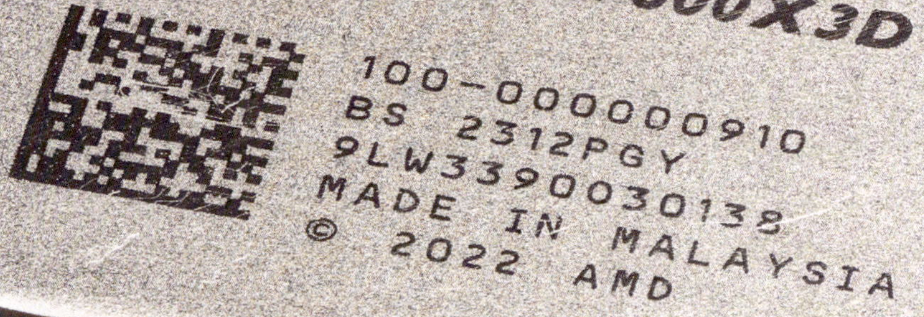
AMD Ryzen 7 7800X3D
100-000000910
BS 2312PGY
9LW3390030138
MADE IN MALAYSIA
© 2022 AMD

CONTENTS

Introduction

In a high-security room on the edge of Silicon Valley, California, the world's fastest **supercomputer**, El Capitan, is hard at work keeping America's nuclear weapons safe. The room that houses El Capitan is as big as two tennis courts, side by side. Inside, on more than 87 shelves and with 90 miles of cable, 44,000 **chips** called accelerated processing units (**APUs**) perform calculations so fast that, according to TIME magazine, if everyone on

OPPOSITE: Construction of the El Capitan supercomputer was completed in November 2024. It was built as part of the U.S. Department of Energy's efforts to support national security through advanced simulation.

Earth were to make one calculation per second, it would take them over 480 years to do in a minute what El Capitan can do in sixty seconds. Put another way, the machine is fast enough to carry out 1 quintillion operations per second.

The maker of these chips? A technology company called Advanced Micro Devices, or AMD. Thanks to its CEO, Dr. Lisa Su, AMD has become one of the greatest success stories in American history, working with companies like Microsoft, Meta, Google, and many others to power supercomputers, computers, video games, healthcare systems, business applications, cars, aerospace, AI innovations, and more.

So, when Lisa heard the news in November 2024 that the most powerful supercomputer in the world was running on AMD chips, she was thrilled. It was proof that

Lawrence Livermore National Lab, home of El Capitan

AMD products were making a difference in the world. "These are the days I live for," she said in an interview, adding that the chips in El Capitan are "without a doubt, the most complex thing we've ever built."

But in a world that's advancing so quickly, and where new regulations, trade wars, and competitors are a constant threat, can AMD continue to advance the computer technology industry and transform the future?

AMD
AMD

Memory Lane

AMD's story begins long before computers were part of our daily lives. In fact, it begins before the **semiconductor** industry existed—when the world hadn't yet dreamed of things like **microprocessors**, servers, personal computers (PCs), laptops, gaming consoles, **data centers**, and supercomputers; before Microsoft, Meta, and Google; and before entire economies, national security, healthcare, scientific research, the

OPPOSITE: In the 1980s and '90s, Jerry Sanders turned AMD into a brash competitor to Intel with a mix of savvy, bold marketing, and by creating a sense of fierce loyalty within the company.

automotive industry, space travel, and artificial intelligence relied on computer chips to process information, solve problems, and tackle the challenges of the future.

AMD, which stands for Advanced Micro Devices, was co-founded in 1969 by visionary engineer and businessman Walter Jeremiah Sanders III. Jerry Sanders, as he's known, was born in 1936 in Chicago, Illinois. His parents divorced when he was four, so he was raised by his father's parents. He didn't have the easiest upbringing. Once, as a teenager, he was beaten up so badly by a street gang that he nearly died. He wasn't treated well at home, either. Jerry's grandfather was not encouraging—he used to tell Jerry that he would never amount to anything. But Jerry was smart, charismatic, and full of character, so he set out to prove his grandfather wrong. He earned an academic scholarship and graduated from the University of Illinois in 1958 with a degree in electrical engineering.

Jerry was a good salesperson and worked at Douglas Aircraft Company and Motorola before moving to California's Silicon Valley to work at Fairchild Semiconductor in 1961. Fairchild was one of the first companies to develop the building blocks that would revolutionize the electronics industry. Its engineers pioneered **transistors** (which control electrical signals) and integrated circuits—or **microchips** (small, complex electrical devices)—in the computers, smartphones and televisions in use today. Known collectively

EXIT

OPPOSITE Fairchild Semiconductor, 1964

as semiconductors, these innovations enable devices to process and store information. Though Jerry could never have imagined what the future would hold, he believed in semiconductors and in the company's plans to change the world. "It was magic," said Jerry, looking back on his time at Fairchild "There's never been anything like it before, never been anything like it since."

A few years after joining Fairchild Semiconductor, the company's new CEO fired Jerry and several other employees. Now jobless, Jerry rented a beach house in Malibu and took some time to think. It was during this period that Jerry and eight other Fairchild engineers agreed to start their own company, called AMD. Even though he humorously remarked that he "was a baby" when he started the company, Jerry was named its first President. Meanwhile, several other engineers from Fairchild left at the same time as Jerry—they also started a computer company called Intel, which would become a major AMD rival. While Intel secured funding quickly, it took AMD six months to get startup money. Jerry even had to sleep on other people's couches until investors—bolstered by some seed money from Intel's founder Robert Noyce—helped AMD raise the $1.5 million it needed to get started. No matter what it would take, "I'm determined to fulfill my dream," Jerry said in an

Robert Noyce

A New Kind of Company

Advanced Micro Devices wasn't the company's first choice of names. In fact, it was 17th on the list—the other 16 had already been trademarked. Still, the name suited the company well. Its founders wanted to create new opportunities for semiconductor products—products that could change the world. And that change began within the company itself. AMD offered its employees stock options and ensured that everyone shared in the company's success. Jerry refused to lay off staff during hard times. During good times, he handed out cash and cheques so that everyone could enjoy the profits. On one occasion, he even raffled off a house. He wanted to treat employees fairly.

interview. At the time, many said the company wouldn't be a success. "I made it happen..." he added proudly.

The company set up its headquarters in Santa Clara, part of Silicon Valley, in the back of a carpet-cutting company. AMD started out by making semiconductor products such as **memory chips**, integrated circuits, microprocessors, and other computer parts. Since other companies were also producing semiconductors, AMD distinguished itself by manufacturing high-quality, reliable products that met military standards—good enough to be used by the military and aerospace industries. This guaranteed the integrity of their products at a time when other semiconductors did not always perform reliably. Sales increased so much that AMD became a public company in 1972 and built a manufacturing facility in Malaysia.

Jerry had big plans. He wanted AMD to become one of the largest semiconductor manufacturers by 1975—even though, at the time, AMD wasn't even in the top 10. AMD kept growing and producing more products. By 1978, sales totaled more than $100 million. AMD was named one of the 100 Best Companies to Work For in America and made the Fortune 500 list for the first time in 1985. Despite the ups and downs of the economy and battles with its rival Intel over **market share** and licensing agreements, AMD continued to expand and innovate, all while maintaining a strong focus on collaboration and employee well-being. In 2002, after 33 years at the helm, Jerry stepped down as CEO.

By the early 2010s, things at AMD weren't going so well. The company was bleeding money, and some of its business decisions hadn't paid off as expected. The global recession in 2008 and 2009 forced AMD to cut 1,100 jobs—something Jerry would have opposed. New CEOs came and went, and by 2012, further layoffs—representing a quarter of AMD's total workforce—were

Dr. Lisa Su, announced as CEO of AMD in 2014

announced. AMD's stock price had plummeted to around $2, which made it nearly worthless.

Yet AMD's fortunes were about to change. In 2014, AMD announced that Dr. Lisa Su would be its new President and CEO. Lisa, a brilliant Taiwanese-born, MIT-educated electrical engineer, had already been with the company for two years. But with the company at a crossroads, Lisa faced some big decisions.

"In 2014–15, when I first took over as CEO," said Lisa, "people were excited about the next Apple iPhone or tablet. My board was asking me, 'Why aren't we in phones and tablets?'" Lisa explained that while those were fine businesses, they were not what AMD was about. "The key is to be very clear on what we want to be the best at. It doesn't have to be the most popular thing, but it has to be something that you know will make a difference."

About Silicon Valley

Silicon Valley, in Northern California, is the global center of innovation and technology. It's home to thousands of startups and major tech giants like Apple, Google, Netflix, Meta, Intel, Nvidia, and AMD. The name, first used in the 1970s, comes from silicon—the material used in microchips that power modern technology.

Lisa went all in, focusing on high-performance computing and making the chips that power some of the world's biggest companies and most important industries. "You need chips in everything you do, in every part of life and business," she said. "Touching billions of people with AMD technology would be a wonderful thing."

In the years since taking the helm, Lisa has turned AMD into a great success story. But how did she do it? What does AMD do now? And how is the company impacting the world?

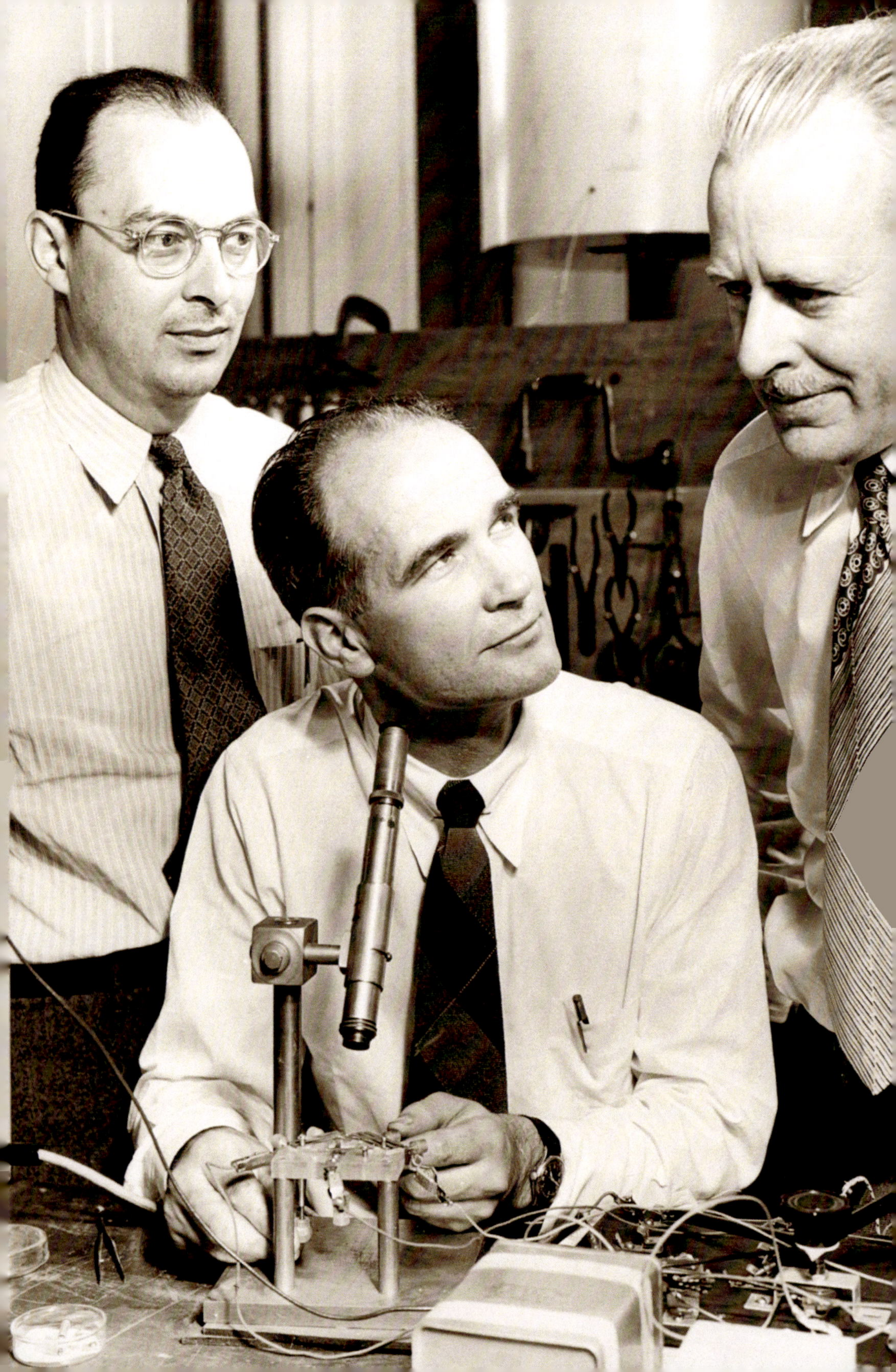

AMD

A Gargantuan Task

Over the last several decades, the world's most powerful economies, countries, and companies have been transformed by semiconductors—or chips. Chips are the brains behind computers, phones, cars, the internet, banking, science, and AI tools like ChatGPT. People can't send emails, shop online, scroll through social

OPPOSITE: John Bardeen, William Shockley and Walter Brattain developed the bipolar point-contact transistor in 1947.

media, play video games, drive a car, or chat with an AI assistant online without this technology. All of these things rely on computers, which run on chips that are now smaller, faster, and more efficient than ever. Anyone who looked inside their vehicles or personal computers would likely find an AMD chip. Lisa has played a big role in making that possible.

Lisa immigrated to New York from Taiwan when she was three years old. Lisa's parents wanted her and her brother to be successful and encouraged them to study math and science. Their dad even used to ask them math questions at the dining room table. Lisa loved solving problems, so she was excited to help her brother when his remote control car stopped working. She took the device apart, found the faulty wire, and put it back together again. Problem solved!

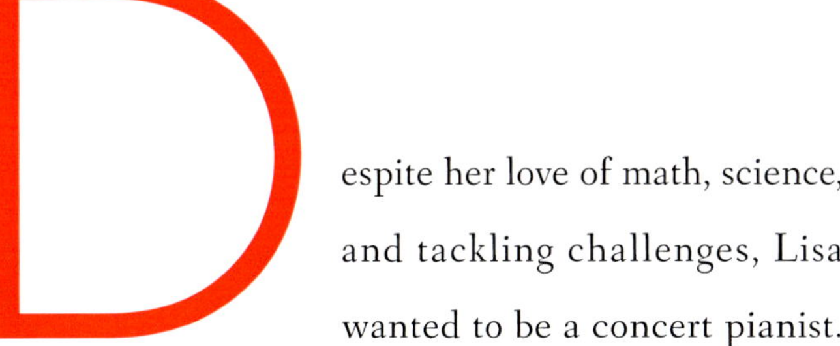

Despite her love of math, science, and tackling challenges, Lisa wanted to be a concert pianist. When she realized she wasn't good enough, she set her sights on attending university. After high school, Lisa attended the Massachusetts Institute of Technology (MIT) and studied electrical engineering, earning her bachelor's, master's, and PhD degrees there. She says she

Lisa Su's doctoral work focused on silicon-on-insulator (SOI) technology, which later became foundational in chip design.

chose electrical engineering because it was the hardest subject she could study. She secured a research job and a window into the world of semiconductors the summer after her freshman year.

Fascinated by the process of making chips and by the problem-solving potential of semiconductors, Lisa was sold. "It was so cool to me," she said in an interview. "Semiconductors are so interesting because I could make something that worked." She was amazed to learn how new innovations like copper interconnects to make chips work faster and with less power. "Much of the challenge was how you could keep increasing performance and capability while making devices smaller, so you could put more transistors on a single chip."

After graduating, Lisa worked at Texas Instruments and IBM, where she learned how to manage teams and run a business. "I was really lucky early in my career," said Lisa. "Every two years, I did a different thing." All that experience at other tech companies was invaluable. "I felt like I was in training for the opportunity to do something meaningful in the semiconductor industry," she said. "And AMD was my shot."

When she joined AMD as the Senior Vice President and General Manager, Global Business Units in 2012, Lisa was impressed by the company's technology and its incredible talent. It was the perfect combination. "I love running good businesses, and most importantly, I love being able to bring great products to the market." Joining AMD felt "natural." It was a chance to do something important—something that mattered. "It's always been about that for me. How do we get the next generation of processors out there? Or the best visualization capabilities?"

When she received a phone call telling her that the company wanted her to be President and CEO in 2014, she was

Everyone Loves Lisa

Lisa Su laughingly calls herself a technology geek. So, what exactly does that mean for Lisa? When she gets up in the morning, she reads the news and Reddit threads, and she even runs ChatGPT. She loves reading feedback about AMD products—good and bad. Her favorite place to vacation is Cabo, Mexico, because she loves the beaches and golfing. Now a billionaire, Lisa has received many awards and honors, including being named TIME magazine's CEO of the Year and Financial Times Woman of the Year in 2024. Always an optimist, Lisa believes that AMD's staff are so smart they can solve any problem—especially if they work with others. Lisa and her husband live in Austin, Texas.

excited. For Lisa, this was "an opportunity of a lifetime." The business was in disarray and she faced what was called a "gargantuan task." Executives had rounded stock prices down to $0. Lisa remained unfazed. "So few companies have what AMD has to offer...I'm extremely excited about everything we can do together."

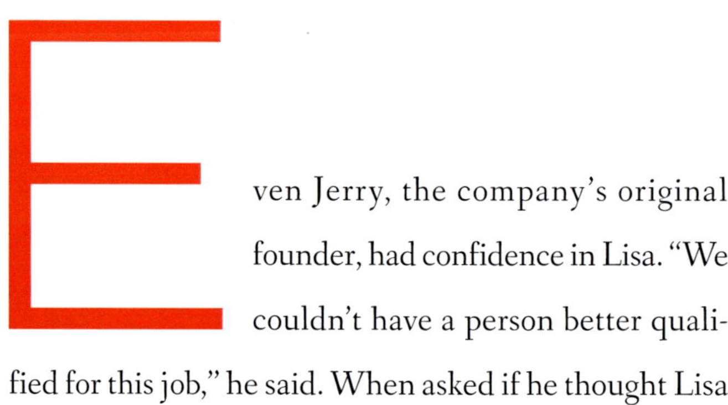

Even Jerry, the company's original founder, had confidence in Lisa. "We couldn't have a person better qualified for this job," he said. When asked if he thought Lisa could one day beat AMD's biggest rival, Nvidia, Jerry answered, "Not a question in my mind."

From the beginning, Lisa had a clear vision. "My dream as CEO is to make us a great company—a company with products we're proud of."

Although board members initially wanted Lisa to pursue less powerful chips, she chose a different path. She focused on building top-tier chips and data centers, to help solve customer problems, and empower AMD engineers to innovate. Known for her high standards, Lisa embodied a unique blend of people skills and technical expertise. If anyone were capable of turning AMD around, her employees, stockholders, customers, and partners believed Lisa was the right person for the job.

Her plan worked. Lisa oversaw the redesign of AMD's products and repaired relationships with customers like Meta and Google. “We had to get large partners to trust us and trust that we could develop the best technology in the world to power their business with our technology,” said Lisa.

In 2022, AMD surpassed its longtime rival Intel in market value for the first time. In addition, AMD’s stock price increased by nearly 50 times, to about $140 a share. And, of course, AMD chips power El Capitan, the world’s fastest exascale supercomputer.

Relatives and Rivalries

Despite its success, AMD isn't the top semiconductor company in the world. In fact, Lisa's cousin, Jensen Huang, runs that business—Nvidia. But Lisa is a competitive person who loves to win, so there's no telling which family member may end up ahead. Meanwhile, AMD's age-old competitor, Intel, has had some problems. Its stock prices are well below AMD's, and its share of the chip market decreased while AMD"s grew. When AMD became worth more than Intel in 2022, one executive said, "It felt fantastic. It's something that I don't think anybody in the industry would have believed was possible just a few years ago."

Business experts call it "one of the great turnaround stories of modern American business history."

But Lisa wasn't done yet. As she looked to the future, she wondered, "How do we do something nobody else can do?"

To that end, she bet on AI as the future. "I believe AI is the most important technology I've seen in my career," said Lisa, who in 2022 began making chips to run AI systems—creating new billion-dollar business opportunities for the company. "We're at the very, very beginning of AI. Whatever you think you're doing today

AMD Athlon™
AXDA2600DKV3C 9487594260050
AIUHB 0246XPAW ⓜ © 1999 AMD

OPPOSITE Modern computer chips can contain over 100 billion transistors.

that seems amazing will be 10 times more amazing twelve months from now."

At the same time, challenges lie ahead. AMD remains a strong competitor, though it trails well behind its rival Nvidia. Some partners are starting to make their own chips. A trade war with China, or a possible Chinese takeover of Taiwan where AMD's chips are made could deal AMD a direct blow.

When the Chips Are Down

When Lisa became head of AMD in 2014, the company needed money immediately. Over the next few years, she signed deals with video game console manufacturers and with several Chinese companies that wanted to use AMD designs to make computer processors for the Chinese market. That brought in even more money.

But since then, AMD's decision to work with Chinese companies could backfire. According to reports, the Pentagon tried to block AMD's deal with China in 2016 but couldn't. Pentagon officials worried that AMD had given China important information that would help it develop the best semiconductors. AMD says it didn't do anything wrong and that all the laws were followed. Today, U.S.–China tensions have escalated into a trade war, with tariffs on imports and exports and restrictions on which chips can be sold to China. The U.S. aims to keep the most advanced American chip designs out of Chinese hands to maintain a competitive edge.

"It was a very different era," Lisa said of AMD's deals with China. It was only after those deals that new laws stopped the transfer of important technologies to

Chinese President Xi Jinping

certain foreign governments, and possible risk America's safety. Even newer laws make it illegal for companies like AMD and Nvidia to sell their most advanced chips to Chinese companies. These laws hurt profits, but AMD may be better shielded than firms with deeper ties to countries like China.

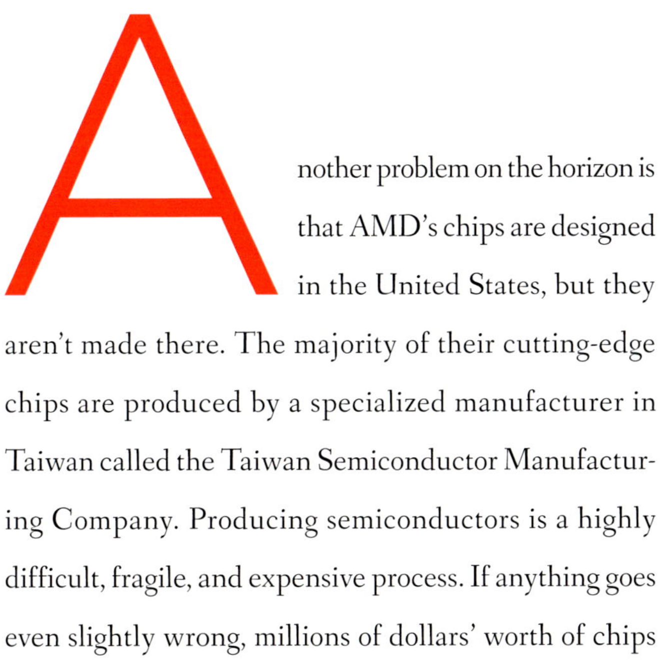

Another problem on the horizon is that AMD's chips are designed in the United States, but they aren't made there. The majority of their cutting-edge chips are produced by a specialized manufacturer in Taiwan called the Taiwan Semiconductor Manufacturing Company. Producing semiconductors is a highly difficult, fragile, and expensive process. If anything goes even slightly wrong, millions of dollars' worth of chips are ruined. Few companies can handle the job, and the world's supply of semiconductors relies on Taiwan's manufacturing capabilities. Why is this a problem?

ews reports suggest that China's president may have plans to invade Taiwan in the near future. China's president says that Taiwan, a self-governing island, belongs to China. The country wants to produce the most advanced semiconductors itself and not rely on companies in the United States, like AMD. A takeover

This image was used by IntelBroker as a profile picture

Who is Intelbroker?

A notorious cybercriminal called Intelbroker is behind many high-profile data leaks. Using sophisticated strategies, Intelbroker has broken into the servers of high-tech companies like AMD, the Los Angeles International Airport, and a U.S. federal technology consulting company called Acuity. Then they post screenshots of the data they've stolen on hacker sites like BreachForums. Why would anyone steal and post sensitive information? Hackers might try to sell stolen information for money, or they might want to hurt the companies or governments involved because of their own beliefs or agendas. One thing is for sure—by exposing vulnerabilities in computer networks, experts can work to outsmart hackers and ensure that company and government data remains secure.

Lisa Su testifies before congress

of Taiwan would give China access to the largest supply of chips in the world.

That would be terrible for the United States. According to Time magazine, "if Beijing's effort to become a world-leading semiconductor producer is successful, it would set up China's military and AI industry to match or outpace America's, which many in Washington view as a national-security threat."

As Lisa explained, "chips are the backbone of everything you do." During the pandemic, that became clear. People couldn't get enough chips—it meant they couldn't manufacture cars or computers. Prices went up, and businesses were at a standstill. For that reason, and for national security, it's become "super important" to make chips in the U.S.

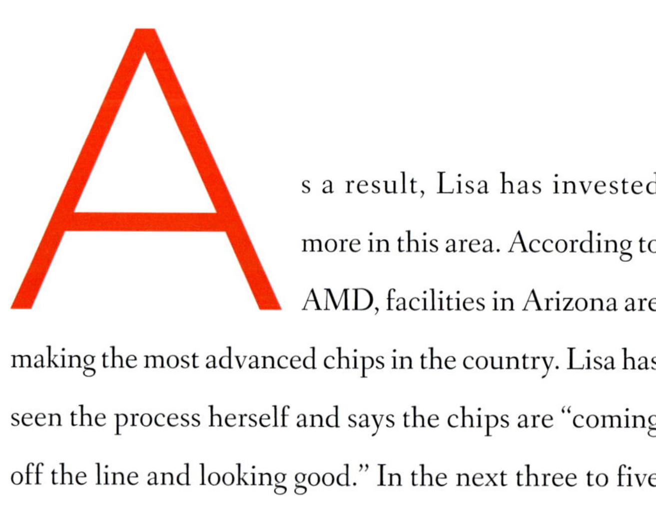

s a result, Lisa has invested more in this area. According to AMD, facilities in Arizona are making the most advanced chips in the country. Lisa has seen the process herself and says the chips are "coming off the line and looking good." In the next three to five years, she expects that the most advanced chips will be made in the United States. Lisa says progress "is going faster than we thought."

All this worry has led some major AI companies to design their own chips. That could affect AMD's profits in the future. But Lisa actually sees this as an opportunity. After all, not many companies have the AMD's $6 billion research and development budget. She thinks companies will buy AMD chips for some tasks and use their own chips for others. "There's no one-size-fits-all in computing," said Lisa. "The broader the **ecosystem**, the bigger the party."

While dealing with issues of profits, competition, and chip manufacturing, AMD has also faced other challenges. In 2019, it settled a class-action lawsuit over advertising for one of its products, the Bulldozer processor. AMD

Computers and Climate Change

Some people worry that all this computing power is harmful to the planet. After all, doesn't it take a lot of energy to power the chips that make advances in technology—advances like AI—possible? AMD believes that next-generation chip technologies will actually help address climate change. Newer and better chips will enable computers to perform more calculations faster, so that less energy is consumed. These calculations can also help solve problems within days or weeks, rather than months or years. Their goal is to produce products that create more computing power with less energy, which is better for the planet.

had advertised this product as being more powerful than one of Intel's, and a judge sided with customers. AMD agreed to pay $12.1 million to users who had purchased the Bulldozer product. AMD was happy to put the issue to rest. The company released a statement saying, "AMD is pleased to have reached a settlement of this lawsuit. While we believe the allegations are without merit, we also believe that eliminating the distraction and settling the litigation is in our best interest."

In fact, the company needs to focus its energy on two other problems. In August 2024, AMD revealed it had discovered a security flaw that affected many **generations** of certain processors. Called Sinkhole, it would enable **hackers** to install **malware** on people's computers. AMD released fixes (**firmware**) and encouraged users to update their servers to protect their data.

Hackers and cyberattacks pose a real threat. In 2022, AMD was targeted by a hacker called RansomHouse, which claimed to have stolen information from AMD's networks. In 2024, a hacker called Intelbroker said it had also taken information from AMD. In this **data leak**, the hackers stole employee details, software code, financial records, and more. This is a major issue that puts the company's designs and profits at risk. If

AMD cryptocurrency mining unit

people can't trust AMD to be safe and secure from hackers, nobody will want to work with the company or buy its products. Officials take these breaches seriously. Leaks are investigated with help from cybersecurity agencies, and new and improved security measures are implemented to outsmart cyber hackers and ensure that top-secret information cannot be stolen again.

Shaping the Future

AMD turned a corner when Lisa became CEO and made bold strategic decisions that paid off. She says that one of the turning points was the redesign of a high-performance chip—what AMD named the Zen chips. First released in 2017, the new Zen design gave AMD a range of innovative chips that could be used in desktop, server, and mobile processors. They performed better, processed data

OPPOSITE: Instead of one big chip, Zen CPUs use multiple smaller ones (chiplets), By using multiple small chiplets, AMD can produce more working chips from each batch and easily build processors with different power levels and sizes.

more quickly, and could calculate a remarkable amount of information simultaneously. AMD began to eat away at Intel's market share, and its stock began to climb.

Lisa's next bet for the future: AI. So far, this choice is paying off too—earning AMD billions of dollars in revenue and opening a market that hadn't existed for the company before. In fact, the AI chip market is predicted to grow to $500 billion by 2028—more than the value of the whole semiconductor industry was 10 years ago.

"I truly believe that AI is the most transformational technology I've seen in my career," said Lisa. She believes it's bigger than other advances that have revolutionized the world, including the internet, PCs, cell phones, and the cloud. "I think AI actually surpasses all that. The rate and pace of change in the industry is faster than anything we've ever seen."

Victor Peng, president ofAMD

OPPOSITE Lisa Su and U.S. Energy Secretary Rick Perry

Her company is on the cutting edge of the latest chip technology. Not only does AMD produce the fastest gaming chips in the world, called X3D, but it also produces some of the most advanced AI chips, called M1300. These chips run the AI workload for companies like Microsoft, GPT, and Meta.

The fact that AMD has become so successful isn't surprising to Lisa. "AMD has had a history of doing amazing things, and from that standpoint, we've always been in a place where we haven't had the same number of people as larger companies—but we've certainly punched above our weight in terms of technological capability and impact on the industry."

AMD wants to use its technology to make a difference in many areas. For starters, Lisa wants to ensure that the next generation of students studies science, technology,

AMD Gives Back

The AMD Foundation invests time, money, and technology into helping local communities. The Foundation donates to disaster relief efforts, supports community projects, and assists with conservation efforts. AMD also matches funds raised by employees, all of which go to local causes. Recently, more than 5,700 AMD employees volunteered over 25,000 hours to put together STEM education kits, plant trees, clean parks, build affordable housing, and provide meals for families without enough food. In Europe alone, staff recently increased their volunteer hours by 90 percent. AMD was even named one of the 100 Best Corporate Citizens of 2024 in recognition of its commitment to environmental, social, and governance issues.

“WE’VE CERTAINLY PUNCHED ABOVE OUR WEIGHT IN TERMS OF TECHNOLOGICAL CAPABILITY AND IMPACT ON THE INDUSTRY”

engineering, and math (STEM). AMD created Learning Labs that provide hardware and AMD expertise to schools and organizations far and wide. Their goal is to inspire students to use this technology to become the innovators, researchers, leaders, and entrepreneurs who discover new ways to solve society’s toughest challenges. AMD has Learning Labs in the U.S. and also in places like China, Malaysia, Ireland, Canada, and Singapore, where they teach coding, robotics, game design, and computer science to students who are disadvantaged in some way.

Lisa actively encourages girls to pursue tech careers. AMD has a special program called Technovation Girls. Geared toward girls ages 8–18, this 12-week program teaches girls to code and create mobile apps to tackle real-world problems, such as mental health and computer safety. Teams then compete on an international stage and can win great prizes. AMD also provides skill training so that underprivileged and vulnerable women in India can get jobs. So far, more than 1,200 women ages 18 to 35 have participated in the program. Meanwhile, a special fellowship program gives girls from lower-income backgrounds access to education so they can improve

Lisa Su is devoted to bringing more women into technology based careers.

AMD

The company's logo—a stylized "A" with an upward arrow—symbolizes progress and innovation.

RGB_HEADER1
CPU_OPT
OPTIMEM
JR1
X57KE
0407
A02
SOCKET1331
AMD
RYZEN
SOCKET AM4
DIMM_B1
DIMM_B2
DIMM_A1
DIMM_A2
STRIX X570-E GAMING
SPI_TPM
CHA_FAN1

their futures. "We've made a lot of progress, but there's a lot more to do," said Lisa.

AMD also prioritizes advancing health care. In 2025, AMD announced a special partnership with a company called Absci, whose mission is to discover new drugs to help cure diseases. AMD also invested $20 million in the company to help it grow. "At Absci, we are always looking for ways to push the boundaries of what's possible in drug discovery," said the CEO of Absci. "This partnership with AMD gives us the unique advantage of working closely with a partner that is deeply committed to supporting our needs while providing the most efficient, innovative AI solutions available." AMD was happy to put its high-performance computers to work at Absci, helping accelerate the pace of new breakthroughs. Using AI software, AMD can help researchers calculate more information faster and at a lower cost than ever before. They hope this will help leading scientists test theories, run simulations, and find cures to major health challenges.

Helping the planet is another important area of focus. Not only do AMD staff around the world celebrate Earth Day by pitching in to help the planet, but they also commit to solving some big environmental goals. The company has increased the energy efficiency of its technology—used to power servers for AI training and high-performance computing—by 30 times. It also has a plan to reduce the greenhouse gas emissions produced by its operations by 50 percent by 2030. In addition, the company is working with its suppliers to increase their use of renewable energy. AMD has put its technology to work by helping climate change researchers learn how to reduce the impact of rising temperatures. They are also finding ways for electric vehicles to charge faster and more efficiently so that even more people can buy environmentally friendly cars. AMD is using its products to help predict the weather more reliably so people can prepare for extreme events and save lives. Meanwhile, the company ensures reliable energy sources so people have power during extreme weather outages.

"There's no problem we can't solve if we put the right team on it and work across the ecosystem," Lisa said about all the issues AMD can help tackle through collaboration. She says the best moments occur when experts collaborate to find solutions to problems that people didn't think were possible to solve. What has always been most important to her is making a difference by working in semiconductors.

Lisa's advice for future leaders is to have confidence, take chances, and not worry about failure. "Run toward problems," said Lisa. "Look for the hardest problem to solve and volunteer to help."

AMD is definitely leading by example.

AMD and F1 Racing

AMD is helping technology advance quickly, and the company enjoys that speed—literally. One of AMD's pet projects is designing the most advanced chips for its Formula 1 Mercedes racing team. Since Formula 1 is the most technologically advanced motorsport in the world, AMD's chips give its F1 team the ability to push the limits of speed and performance. Its technology is still in the early stages, but its chips help engineers make adjustments to their cars. Together, they are learning and adjusting one race at a time. Of course, their car is a special AMD color—graphite blue metallic!

Selected Bibliography

"2024 CEO of the Year Lisa Su," Time Magazine, December 2024, https://time.com/7200909/ceo-of-the-year-2024-lisa-su/

"AMD's CEO Wants to Chip Away at Nvidia's Lead," The Circuit with Emily Chang, Bloomberg Originals, https://youtu.be/8Ve5SAFPYZ8?si=x4S7fvAV967OatJ9

"AMD: How It All Began," https://youtu.be/mb53lYjZlNc?si=dFriX-luZpctgsBn

"CEO of the Year Lisa Su Talks Competition and Collaboration in the Semiconductor Industry," *Time*, https://youtu.be/YlokM_4i1i0?si=XdcSdLbzqMiTPrwN

"How Lisa Su Turned Around AMD," *Fortune Magazine*, https://youtu.be/amBe2bofVas?si=gdl97CQtw2yRYmS2

"Intel & AMD: The First 30 Years," https://youtu.be/kZ9ntfjytTI?si=QtHe-QSLF8yFKeXF

Kyrie, Petra, Lisa Su: Architect of Transformation in Silicon Valley - The Rise, Resilience, and Ambitions of AMD's Visionary CEO, Feb. 29 2024.

Lee, Daniel D., Dr. Lisa Su's AMD: Powering the Future of Artifical Intelligence, June 15, 2023.

Glossary

APUs	Accelerated Processing Units are the engine of most modern supercomputers
Chips	small, flat pieces of semiconductor material that have electronic circuits. They are used in devices like computers, smartphones and televisions
CPUs	Central Processing Units are like the brains of any computer and are responsible for reading and interpreting commands and carrying out instructions from the user
Data	facts and information
Data centers	a building that houses computers, servers, storage drives and IT equipment. It stores digital data for companies, including big ones like Google, Meta, Amazon, Microsoft and more
Data leak	a situation when sensitive information is accidentally or purposely exposed
Ecosystem	when technology, data, and businesses work together to benefit customers
Exascale	a type of supercomputing that can make one quintillion calculations per second
Firmware	a type of software built into a computer that can help the computer fix problems, add features and add security patches to protect it from cyber attacks

Generations a progressive or newer version of a product

Malware software designed to disrupt, damage or access a computer system

Market share how much in sales a company makes compared to its competitors. It tells businesses how they're performing compared to other companies

Memory chips a small device that stores information in a computer

Microchips also called chips or integrated circuits, it's a piece of semiconductor material that has electronic circuits

Microprocessors also known as a central processing unit (CPU), it's a single chip that controls the functions of a computer like the brain

Semiconductors also called chips, they are the engines of our computers, phones, cars, internet services, and AI programs. It's made of material that helps conduct electrical current

Supercomputer a powerful computer used for research, AI and other tasks that require big computing. They can make complex calculations and simulations at high speeds, measured in floating-point operations per second (FLOPS)

Transistors a semiconductor device used to amplify or switch electrical signals and power. They are one of the building blocks of modern electronics, which is why they are often considered one of the greatest inventions of the 1900s

Websites

AMD facts for kids, Kiddle Encyclopedia,
https://kids.kiddle.co/AMD
This kid-friendly website explains AMD's history, products, technologies and more.

Global Foundries K-12 activities
https://gf.com/about-us/gf-in-the-community/stem-at-gf/k-12-activities/
This site has engaging, hands-on activities to help learners understand semiconductors, plus links to in-depth videos about how they are made.

It Took 53 Years for AMD to Beat Intel. Here's Why. Wall Street Journal
https://youtu.be/dhv1Ss1aSMU?si=6OiB8MCxW3VkITIR
This video explains how AMD managed to turn around its fortunes and beat its rival Intel.

This CEO Made AMD Billions - Now She Wants To Dominate The Market With AI, Forbes,
https://youtu.be/k-J72u1yQU4?si=G1qc2nA_Qh9Kq64i
This short video features an interview with Lisa Su and shares how she came to lead AMD and AMD's role in the semiconductor industry.

Index